SUMMARY OF KEYS TO EXPERIENCING AZUSA FIRE

Lessons From Revival That Changed The Landscape Of Global Christianity

JEFF OLIVER

RICK JOYNER

CONTENTS

Introduction to "Summary of Keys To Experiencing Azusa Fire"	v
1. "Because They Were the Humblest"	1
2. "William Joseph Seymour"	4
3. "The Bonnie Brae Revival"	8
4. "312 Azusa Street"	12
5. "The Deluge"	16
6. "Parham and Seymour Part Ways"	20
7. "Opposition and Critics"	24
8. "The Revival Spreads"	28
9. "The Angels, Heavenly Choir, Box, Glory, and Flames"	32
10. "Everyday Healings and Notable Miracles"	35
11. "Brother Seymour"	38
12. "The Decline, Second Shower, and Demise"	41
13. "The Azusa Street Legacy"	45
14. "The Pilgrims of Azusa Street"	49
15. "Beginning of a Worldwide Revival"	53
16. "Unlocking Azusa Fire by Rick Joyner"	57
About the Publisher	61

INTRODUCTION TO "SUMMARY OF KEYS TO EXPERIENCING AZUSA FIRE"

※

In the pages of this summary book, "Summary of Keys To Experiencing Azusa Fire," readers are invited to journey through a condensed exploration of Jeff Oliver and Rick Joyner's profound work, "Keys to Experiencing Azusa Fire." This original text delves deep into the heart of one of the most significant religious movements in modern history - the Azusa Street Revival. A pivotal event that reshaped the landscape of Christianity, the Azusa Street Revival is not just a historical phenomenon but a beacon of spiritual transformation and a harbinger of a greater divine movement yet to unfold.

This summary is crafted to provide an accessible and succinct understanding of Joyner's insights and revelations about the Azusa Street Revival. It is designed for those seeking a quick yet comprehensive grasp of the revival's essence, its impact on the global Christian community, and its implications for future spiritual awakenings. Whether you are a scholar, a spiritual seeker, a Christian believer, or simply a curious reader, this summary offers a distilled essence of the original work, ensuring that the core themes and messages are not lost.

Through this summarized edition, readers will encounter the key elements that made the Azusa Street Revival a cornerstone in religious history - its humble beginnings, the extraordinary leadership of William Seymour, the powerful manifestations of the Holy Spirit, and the revival's role as a precursor to an anticipated global spiritual upheaval. The text encapsulates Joyner's perspective on the revival's enduring legacy and its prophetic significance for a future "harvest" – a move of God that is poised to eclipse the wonders experienced at Azusa Street.

"Summary of Keys To Experiencing Azusa Fire" serves as both a homage to a monumental spiritual event and a prophetic insight into what lies ahead in the realm of faith and divine encounters. It is an invitation to understand the past, discern the present, and anticipate the future of Christianity's spiritual journey.

CHAPTER 1

"BECAUSE THEY WERE THE HUMBLEST"

Bible Verse

"The Lord is near to those who have a broken heart, and saves such as have a contrite spirit." - Psalm 34:18

Introduction

This chapter delves into the profound impact of the Azusa Street Revival and its origins, emphasizing the significance of humility in sparking spiritual awakenings. The author connects the historical events and personal testimonies to demonstrate the power of simple faith and obedience in the face of societal and racial challenges.

Word of Wisdom

"Heroes will arise from the dust of obscure and despised circumstances, whose names will be emblazoned on heav-

en's eternal page of fame." - Frank Bartleman

Main Theme

The central theme is the transformative power of the Holy Spirit in the Azusa Street Revival, highlighting the role of humility and the inclusivity of God's work, regardless of social or racial status.

Key Points

- The Azusa Street Revival was a significant event in church history, marked by the Holy Spirit's work.
- Personal testimonies played a crucial role in understanding and documenting the revival.
- Dr. Finis Yoakum's Pisgah Home movement paralleled the revival, focusing on healing and serving the marginalized.
- The revival was characterized by a diverse congregation, transcending racial and social barriers.
- Humility was a key factor in why God chose the Azusa Street group for this revival.
- The revival's impact was recognized even by secular media, highlighting its global significance.

Key Themes

- The Azusa Street Revival emerged not from established churches, but from humble, marginalized groups, emphasizing God's preference for the humble and the outcast.
- The revival was a part of a broader movement of spiritual awakening across various churches and denominations in Los Angeles, demonstrating a widespread hunger for a deeper spiritual experience.
- Testimonies from various participants highlight the profound personal transformations and miracles that occurred, underscoring the revival's spiritual depth and authenticity.
- The revival's emphasis on racial inclusivity and breaking societal barriers was revolutionary for its time, showcasing the unifying power of the Holy Spirit.
- The revival's legacy continues to influence modern Christian movements, illustrating its enduring impact on global Christianity.

Conclusion

The chapter "Because They Were the Humblest" encapsulates the essence of the Azusa Street Revival, demonstrating how God's work often manifests in unexpected places and through humble individuals. It highlights the power of the Holy Spirit in transcending societal norms, uniting people across racial and social divides, and sparking a global movement that continues to resonate in the Christian faith today.

CHAPTER 2

"WILLIAM JOSEPH SEYMOUR"

Bible Verse

"For God chose the foolish things of the world to shame the wise; God chose the weak things of the world to shame the strong." - 1 Corinthians 1:27

Introduction

This chapter provides a detailed biography of William Joseph Seymour, a key figure in the Azusa Street Revival and a pivotal character in the history of Pentecostalism. It outlines his early life, spiritual journey, and the significant events that shaped his ministry, highlighting his humble beginnings and unwavering faith.

Word of Wisdom

"Seymour had the Holy Spirit...and was very humble." - Kent White

Main Theme

The main theme of the chapter is the life and ministry of William Joseph Seymour, illustrating his transition from the son of former slaves to an influential religious leader who played a central role in the spread of Pentecostalism.

Key Points

- William Joseph Seymour was born to former slaves in Louisiana and faced racial and societal challenges.
- Seymour's spiritual journey began in the Methodist Church, leading to his embrace of Holiness teachings.
- He underwent sanctification and felt called to ministry, overcoming illness and adversity.
- Seymour was influenced by various religious movements, including Charles Parham's teachings on speaking in tongues.
- He moved to Houston, where he embraced the Pentecostal message under Parham's mentorship.
- Seymour's move to Los Angeles at the behest of Lucy Farrow and Neely Terry was pivotal in his ministry.

Key Themes

- Seymour's upbringing in post–Civil War Louisiana, marked by poverty and racial

discrimination, shaped his empathetic and inclusive approach to ministry. His early life was a testament to resilience and faith amidst adversity.
- His spiritual development was heavily influenced by the Holiness movement and Methodism, which instilled in him the values of racial inclusivity, spiritual sanctification, and a deep commitment to Christian teachings.
- Seymour's time in Charles Parham's Bible school was transformative, where he encountered and initially resisted the Pentecostal doctrine of speaking in tongues. This experience was crucial in shaping his later ministry.
- The decision to move to Los Angeles, despite hesitations and challenges, demonstrated Seymour's obedience to what he perceived as divine guidance, marking a turning point in his life and the history of Pentecostalism.
- His role in the Azusa Street Revival, characterized by humility and perseverance, not only transformed his own life but also had a profound and lasting impact on Christian Pentecostalism globally.

Conclusion

William Joseph Seymour's journey from a humble background to becoming a central figure in the Pentecostal movement is a powerful testimony to the transformative power of faith and obedience.

His life exemplifies the scriptural truth that God often uses the humble and marginalized to accomplish great works, as seen in the far-reaching impact of the Azusa Street Revival.

CHAPTER 3

"THE BONNIE BRAE REVIVAL"

Bible Verse
"And suddenly there came from heaven a sound like a mighty rushing wind, and it filled the entire house where they were sitting." - Acts 2:2

Introduction

"The Bonnie Brae Revival" chapter narrates the pivotal events leading to the Azusa Street Revival, focusing on William Seymour's arrival in Los Angeles and the initial outpouring of the Holy Spirit in a small house on Bonnie Brae Street.

Word of Wisdom

"No, that happens all the time. That's not a ghost. That's the Holy Ghost reminding us that He's getting ready to do again what He did here before!" - Current owner of the Bonnie Brae House

Main Theme

The main theme is the humble beginnings of the Pentecostal movement in a small house in Los Angeles, where the Holy Spirit was first poured out in a powerful way, leading to the historic Azusa Street Revival.

Key Points

- The early history of Los Angeles set a diverse and dynamic background for the revival.
- William Seymour left Texas for Los Angeles, feeling called to a new ministry in a city ripe for revival.
- Upon arrival in Los Angeles, Seymour faced initial rejection but persevered in prayer and teaching.
- The Holy Spirit was first poured out in the Bonnie Brae House, leading to speaking in tongues and other spiritual manifestations.
- The revival quickly outgrew the small house, attracting large crowds and attention from the community.
- Seymour himself received the baptism in the Holy Spirit, marking a significant milestone in the revival.

"THE BONNIE BRAE REVIVAL"

Key Themes

- Los Angeles in 1906, described as a city of dreams and opportunities, provided a fertile ground for new spiritual movements. This dynamic environment, coupled with the city's racial diversity, set the stage for the groundbreaking Bonnie Brae Revival.
- William Seymour's journey to Los Angeles illustrates a profound faith and obedience to a perceived divine call, despite facing immediate challenges and rejection upon his arrival.
- The initial outpouring of the Holy Spirit at the Bonnie Brae House was a spontaneous, powerful event that defied traditional church norms and racial barriers, reflecting the inclusive nature of the movement.
- The rapid growth of the revival meetings, characterized by miraculous healings, speaking in tongues, and interracial fellowship, highlighted the intense spiritual hunger and openness of the people in Los Angeles.
- Seymour's personal experience of receiving the baptism in the Holy Spirit validated his teachings and propelled him as a central figure in the burgeoning Pentecostal movement.

Conclusion

"The Bonnie Brae Revival" chapter captures a defining moment in Christian history, where a small gathering in Los Angeles became the catalyst for a worldwide Pentecostal movement. The humble beginnings, marked by racial diversity and spiritual fervor, underscore the transformative power of faith and the Holy Spirit's work in breaking down societal barriers and igniting a global revival.

CHAPTER 4
"312 AZUSA STREET"

Bible Verse
"And they devoted themselves to the apostles' teaching and the fellowship, to the breaking of bread and the prayers." - Acts 2:42

Introduction
"312 Azusa Street" chapter describes the early days of the Azusa Street Mission, the physical preparations of the location, the initial meetings, and the powerful spiritual experiences that occurred there, setting the stage for a significant religious movement.

Word of Wisdom

"We had no planned program, nor are we afraid of anarchy or crooked spirits. God the Holy Spirit is able to control and protect His work." - Description of the

Spirit-led services at the Azusa Street Mission.

Main Theme

The main theme is the establishment and early experiences of the Azusa Street Mission in Los Angeles, which became a focal point for the Pentecostal movement, characterized by spontaneous and powerful spiritual manifestations.

Key Points

• Volunteers, including A.G. Osterberg and Sister Carney, worked diligently to prepare the old warehouse for use as a church.

• The first convert at the Azusa Street Mission was a Roman Catholic worker, symbolizing the mission's inclusive and transformative nature.

• The initial setup of the mission included makeshift benches, a simple pulpit, and an area for prayer and healing.

• The first meeting at 312 Azusa Street had a modest attendance, but the congregation quickly grew as word spread.

• The Los Angeles Daily Times published a front-page article on the mission, inadvertently providing free advertising and attracting more attendees.

• The devastating 1906 San Francisco earthquake coincided with the beginning of the revival, heightening the spiritual urgency of the time.

Key Themes

- The humble and cooperative effort to prepare the Azusa Street location demonstrates the grassroots nature of the revival, where people from diverse backgrounds united for a common spiritual purpose.
- The Azusa Street Mission's inclusive approach, welcoming people of all races and backgrounds, was a radical departure from the societal norms of the time and a testament to the mission's commitment to unity in Christ.
- The Spirit-led services at Azusa Street, characterized by spontaneity and a lack of structured programming, reflected a deep reliance on the Holy Spirit's guidance and an openness to diverse spiritual expressions.
- The significant growth of the mission's congregation, driven by word-of-mouth and media attention, highlights the profound impact and appeal of the spiritual experiences occurring there.
- The coincidence of the San Francisco earthquake with the onset of the revival added a sense of divine urgency and symbolism, intertwining a natural disaster with a spiritual awakening.

Conclusion

The chapter "312 Azusa Street" captures a pivotal moment in religious history, where a modestly prepared warehouse became the birthplace of a global

Pentecostal movement. The collective efforts of the volunteers, the spontaneous nature of the services, and the extraordinary spiritual experiences marked the Azusa Street Mission as a unique and powerful catalyst for change and revival.

CHAPTER 5
"THE DELUGE"

Bible Verse
"And they were all filled with the Holy Spirit and began to speak in other tongues as the Spirit gave them utterance." - Acts 2:4

Introduction

"The Deluge" chapter vividly portrays the explosive growth and profound spiritual experiences at the Azusa Street Mission during the summer of 1906. It captures the diverse and intense nature of the revival, emphasizing the unity and miraculous occurrences that transcended cultural and linguistic barriers.

Word of Wisdom

"The breath would be taken from them. Their minds would wander, their brains reel. Things would turn black be-

fore their eyes. They could not go on." - Frank Bartleman, describing the impact of the Holy Spirit on those attempting to disrupt the Azusa Street services.

Main Theme

The chapter highlights the overwhelming influx of people from various backgrounds to the Azusa Street Mission, the extraordinary spiritual manifestations experienced there, and the challenges of discerning genuine from counterfeit spiritual activities.

Key Points

• The Azusa Street Mission drew large, diverse crowds, with attendance reaching up to 1,500 on Sundays.

• Meetings attracted a significant number of pastors and evangelists, contributing to the rapid spread of the revival.

• The revival was marked by instances of people speaking in foreign languages they hadn't learned, affirming the miraculous work of the Holy Spirit.

• Visitors from afar, including missionaries and ministers, came to experience the revival, often led by a strong spiritual draw.

• The mission faced challenges from counterfeit spirits and individuals trying to disrupt or exploit the meetings.

"THE DELUGE"

Key Themes

- The physical space of the Azusa Street Mission became a melting pot of different races and nationalities, united in their pursuit of a deeper spiritual experience. This unprecedented integration during a racially segregated era emphasized the revival's focus on spiritual unity over societal divisions.
- The revival's spontaneous and powerful nature drew scrutiny and criticism from the outside world, but the authenticity of the experiences and the transformations of individuals served as a testament to the genuine work of the Holy Spirit.
- The phenomenon of speaking in unknown languages was a significant feature of the revival, echoing the events of Pentecost in the Book of Acts. This served as both a sign of divine presence and a powerful tool for transcending cultural and linguistic barriers.
- The revival's impact extended far beyond the physical location of the mission, drawing individuals from across the globe. This global pull highlighted the universal appeal and significance of the revival, transcending geographical and cultural boundaries.
- The challenge of discerning genuine spiritual experiences from counterfeit manifestations was a constant theme. Leaders relied on prayer and spiritual discernment to navigate these challenges,

reflecting a deep dependence on the Holy Spirit for guidance.

Conclusion

"The Deluge" chapter encapsulates a pivotal moment in religious history, where the Azusa Street Mission became the epicenter of a global Pentecostal movement. The chapter vividly depicts the mission's transformative impact on individuals from diverse backgrounds and the challenges faced in maintaining the purity and authenticity of the revival amidst external and internal pressures.

CHAPTER 6

"PARHAM AND SEYMOUR PART WAYS"

Bible Verse

"For there is one God and one mediator between God and mankind, the man Christ Jesus." - 1 Timothy 2:5

Introduction

"Parham and Seymour Part Ways" chapter delves into the complex relationship between Charles Parham and William J. Seymour, highlighting their differing approaches to leadership and spiritual discernment during the early Pentecostal movement.

Word of Wisdom

"We can be rather hasty, especially when we are very young in the power of the Holy Spirit. We are just like a baby—full of love—and were willing to accept

anyone that had the baptism with the Holy Spirit as our leader. But the Lord commenced settling us down, and we saw that the Lord should be our leader." - William J. Seymour

Main Theme

The chapter examines the divergent paths of Parham and Seymour, emphasizing their conflicting views on spiritual manifestations, leadership, and interracial cooperation within the Pentecostal movement.

Key Points

• Seymour requested Parham's guidance at Azusa Street, but Parham was occupied with issues in Zion, Illinois.

• Parham's Apostolic Faith Movement had a significantly larger following than Seymour's mission.

• Parham's visit to Los Angeles led to criticism of Azusa Street's spiritual practices and racial integration.

• Parham's efforts in Zion City influenced the convergence of divine healing and Pentecostalism.

• Parham and Seymour's relationship deteriorated due to doctrinal differences and leadership styles.

Key Themes

- The intersection of Parham's and Seymour's ministries reflected a critical juncture in the Pentecostal movement, highlighting issues such as spiritual discernment, race relations, and leadership dynamics. Parham's traditional approach clashed with Seymour's more inclusive and experiential style.
- Parham's decision to prioritize Zion over Azusa had a lasting impact, fostering the spread of Pentecostalism and integrating it with divine healing ministries. This strategic move played a key role in expanding the Pentecostal movement's global influence.
- Parham's visit to Azusa Street revealed stark contrasts in their attitudes towards spiritual manifestations and racial integration, underscoring the evolving nature of Pentecostal theology and practice during this period.
- The divergence in leadership styles between Parham and Seymour - Parham's authoritative and doctrinal approach versus Seymour's more participatory and experiential leadership - illustrated the diversity within early Pentecostalism.
- The breakup between Parham and Seymour symbolized a significant shift in the Pentecostal movement, with Seymour's inclusive approach at Azusa Street paving the way for a more diverse and expansive movement.

Conclusion

The chapter "Parham and Seymour Part Ways" presents a nuanced picture of early Pentecostalism, marked by dynamic leadership, theological debates, and the challenge of nurturing a nascent religious movement amidst diverse viewpoints. The contrasting paths of Parham and Seymour not only shaped the direction of the Pentecostal movement but also highlighted the complexities and challenges inherent in religious leadership and spiritual revival.

CHAPTER 7

"OPPOSITION AND CRITICS"

Bible Verse
"Blessed are you when people insult you, persecute you and falsely say all kinds of evil against you because of me." - Matthew 5:11

Introduction

"Opposition and Critics" explores the myriad challenges and criticisms faced by the Azusa Street Revival, highlighting the external pressures and internal dynamics that shaped the movement.

Word of Wisdom

"Those who have the wisdom to distinguish between the true and the false...have great possibilities of usefulness

before them in this movement." - A.S. Worrell

Main Theme

The chapter sheds light on the skepticism, resistance, and outright hostility encountered by the Azusa Street Revival, reflecting the complex interplay of social, racial, and religious dynamics at the time.

Key Points

• The Azusa Street Revival faced criticism from various religious denominations and societal groups.

• Some local churches lost members to the revival, causing tension and closures.

• Legal and health authorities were called upon to intervene due to perceived disruptions and unsanitary conditions.

• Prominent local leaders and church officials publicly denounced the revival.

• The Azusa Street Mission strove to promote unity amidst a backdrop of criticism and skepticism.

Key Themes

- The Azusa Street Revival's unconventional worship practices and open acceptance of diverse congregants, including interracial gatherings, evoked significant resistance from conservative religious communities and the broader society. This resistance underscores the transformative and boundary-crossing nature of the revival.
- Criticisms of the revival often focused on its perceived fanaticism and chaotic worship style, reflecting broader societal discomfort with expressive religious experiences that challenged established norms.
- Despite opposition, the revival continued to attract a wide range of participants, including respected community members and religious leaders. Their endorsements and conversions added legitimacy to the movement and countered prevailing negative perceptions.
- The revival's emphasis on direct spiritual experiences, such as speaking in tongues, was a focal point of contention, illustrating the tension between traditional religious doctrine and emerging Pentecostal beliefs.
- The Azusa Street Revival's impact extended beyond its immediate locale, influencing broader religious movements and fostering the spread of Pentecostalism, even as it faced persistent criticism and skepticism.

Conclusion

"Opposition and Critics" reveals the Azusa Street Revival as a powerful yet controversial movement that challenged existing religious and social norms. Despite facing significant opposition, the revival's emphasis on spiritual empowerment, racial unity, and a direct relationship with the divine left an enduring mark on the Christian landscape, demonstrating the resilience and transformative power of faith.

CHAPTER 8

"THE REVIVAL SPREADS"

Bible Verse
"And He said to them, 'Go into all the world and preach the gospel to all creation.'" - Mark 16:15
"

Introduction

"The Revival Spreads" chronicles the expansion of the Azusa Street Revival beyond its initial location, as attendees established missions in various locations and spread the revival's message through diverse methods of evangelism.

Word of Wisdom

"One reason for the depth of the work at Azusa was the fact that the workers were not novices. They were largely called and prepared for years from

the Holiness ranks and from the mission field, and so on." - Frank Bartleman

Main Theme

The chapter illustrates the rapid spread of the Azusa Street Revival, emphasizing the role of committed evangelists in propagating the movement through street evangelism, creation of affiliated missions, and ecumenical outreach.

Key Points

- Affiliated missions and revival efforts rapidly expanded in Los Angeles and beyond.

- Street evangelism became a key method for spreading the revival, often leading to dramatic encounters and legal challenges.

- Streetcar evangelism facilitated the movement's outreach, utilizing the city's transit system to access wider audiences.

- Water baptism services were significant events, attracting large crowds and symbolizing public commitment.

- The Azusa Street staff, comprised of volunteers and dedicated leaders, played a crucial role in organizing and sustaining the revival's momentum.

Key Themes

- The expansion of the revival into various cities and neighborhoods demonstrated the revival's appeal across different communities, showcasing its ability to attract diverse groups of people, from various socio-economic backgrounds.
- Street evangelism, characterized by bold public preaching and singing, often led to confrontations with authorities but also remarkable conversions, underscoring the evangelists' commitment and the movement's transformative impact.
- The strategic use of the streetcar system for evangelism highlights the revival's adaptability and resourcefulness in utilizing available infrastructure to maximize outreach efforts.
- Large-scale water baptism services, often held at beaches, became a hallmark of the revival, symbolizing the participants' new spiritual birth and commitment to the movement.
- The leadership and staff at Azusa Street, including key figures like Seymour, Smith, Sargent, Moore, and Crawford, provided essential organizational support, ensuring the revival's message was effectively disseminated and its activities well-coordinated.

Conclusion

"The Revival Spreads" portrays the Azusa Street Revival as a dynamic and influential religious movement that rapidly extended its reach through innovative evangelism and committed leadership. The chapter highlights the revival's ability to transcend traditional boundaries, embrace diversity, and foster a sense of unity among its participants, leaving a lasting legacy in the history of Christianity.

CHAPTER 9

"THE ANGELS, HEAVENLY CHOIR, BOX, GLORY, AND FLAMES"

Bible Verse

"Praise him with the sound of the trumpet: praise him with the psaltery and harp." - Psalm 150:3

Introduction

This chapter delves into the unique worship and spiritual experiences at the Azusa Street Revival, highlighting the emergence of new hymns, spontaneous singing in tongues, and the manifestation of heavenly phenomena.

Word of Wisdom

"A spiritual atmosphere must be created, through humility and prayer, that Satan cannot live in." - Frank Bartleman

Main Theme

The chapter explores the profound and often supernatural worship practices at the Azusa Street Revival, including singing in tongues, the appearance of angels, and the manifestation of heavenly glory and flames.

Key Points

• The revival featured a mix of traditional hymns and spontaneous singing in tongues.

• Worship sessions often included no song leaders or instruments, relying on Spirit-led spontaneity.

• Participants reported seeing and hearing angels, adding a mystical dimension to the meetings.

• The Russian Molokans' participation aligned with their own traditional worship practices.

• The "heavenly choir" and singing in tongues were central to the revival's worship experience.

Key Themes

- The worship at Azusa Street was characterized by a departure from traditional, structured hymn singing to a more spontaneous, Spirit-led form. This shift, while controversial, was believed to allow a more genuine connection with the divine.
- Reports of supernatural occurrences, such as the presence of angels and heavenly

choirs, underscored the revival's emphasis on direct, mystical experiences with the divine, setting it apart from more conventional religious practices.

Conclusion

"The Angels, Heavenly Choir, Box, Glory, and Flames" captures the essence of the Azusa Street Revival's unique approach to worship and spirituality. The blend of traditional hymns with spontaneous, Spirit-led singing, along with supernatural phenomena, created a deeply mystical and transformative atmosphere. This chapter not only documents these extraordinary events but also highlights the revival's impact on contemporary worship practices.

CHAPTER 10

"EVERYDAY HEALINGS AND NOTABLE MIRACLES"

Bible Verse

"And these signs will accompany those who believe: In my name they will drive out demons; they will speak in new tongues; they will pick up snakes with their hands; and when they drink deadly poison, it will not hurt them at all; they will place their hands on sick people, and they will get well." - Mark 16:17-18

Introduction

This chapter looks into the extraordinary healings and miracles that occurred daily at the Azusa Street Revival. It highlights the profound impact of prayer and faith in producing physical healings and deliverances, emphasizing the revival's commitment to divine intervention in everyday life.

"EVERYDAY HEALINGS AND NOTABLE MIRACLES"

Word of Wisdom

"Thank God we have a living Christ among us to heal our diseases. He will heal every case." - Seymour

Main Theme

The chapter details the regular occurrence of miraculous healings at the Azusa Street Revival, from curing physical ailments to casting out demons, demonstrating the revival's deep belief in and reliance on the supernatural power of God.

Key Points

- Prayer sessions in the upper room resulted in numerous people receiving divine healing and the baptism in the Holy Spirit.

- Individuals with serious illnesses experienced miraculous recoveries, often instantaneously.

- Azusa Street services saw regular occurrences of physical healings, including the restoration of hearing, sight, and mobility.

- Miracles of deliverance from demonic possession were common, highlighting the spiritual depth of the revival.

- The youth of Azusa Street played a significant role in praying for and witnessing these miracles.

Key Themes

- The diverse range of healings, from minor ailments to life-threatening diseases, underscored a deep faith in the healing power of Jesus Christ and His promise to heal all who believe.
- The spontaneous nature of many miracles, often occurring without prior arrangement or expectation, reinforced the belief in the constant presence and intervention of the Holy Spirit in the daily activities of the revival.

Conclusion

"Everyday Healings and Notable Miracles" offers a compelling narrative of the Azusa Street Revival's impact through its manifestation of divine healings and miracles. It not only captures the essence of the revival's faith in God's healing power but also showcases the profound transformations experienced by individuals from all walks of life. This chapter serves as a testament to the revival's legacy in demonstrating the tangible presence of God's power in the world.

CHAPTER 11

"BROTHER SEYMOUR"

Bible Verse

"But the fruit of the Spirit is love, joy, peace, forbearance, kindness, goodness, faithfulness, gentleness and self-control." - Galatians 5:22-23

Introduction

This chapter provides an in-depth look at William Seymour, the beloved leader of the Azusa Street Revival. It highlights his humility, spiritual depth, and the profound respect he commanded among those at the revival.

Word of Wisdom

"Love, Faith, Unity are our watchwords, and 'Victory through the Atoning Blood' our battle cry." - William Seymour

Main Theme

The chapter focuses on Seymour's character, leadership style, and his impact on the Azusa Street Revival. It portrays him as a humble, godly man with a deep spiritual connection that drew people to him and to the revival.

Key Points

• William Seymour was known for his humility, often unwittingly carrying donations in his pockets.

• His powerful voice and preaching style were instrumental in attracting people to the Azusa Street Revival.

• Seymour was described as gentle, unassuming, and endowed with a divine anointing.

• His emphasis on ecumenism and unity among Christians was a key aspect of his ministry.

• Seymour believed in the power of the Holy Spirit to lead the church, rather than human authority.

Key Themes

- Seymour's preaching focused on the simplicity of the gospel, emphasizing salvation, sanctification, and the baptism of the Holy Spirit. His teachings stressed the importance of a life transformed by the Holy Spirit, marked by love and humility.
- Despite not being a dynamic orator, Seymour's sermons were impactful, often bringing about profound spiritual

experiences among listeners. His messages were characterized by their directness and emphasis on the necessity of divine love.

Conclusion

"Brother Seymour" captures the essence of a man who was pivotal to the Azusa Street Revival. His gentle yet powerful leadership, combined with a deep commitment to the workings of the Holy Spirit, created an environment where many experienced profound spiritual transformations. Seymour's legacy is one of humility, love, and a deep reliance on God, setting a standard for spiritual leadership and unity in the Christian community.

CHAPTER 12

"THE DECLINE, SECOND SHOWER, AND DEMISE"

Bible Verse

"For where envy and self-seeking exist, confusion and every evil thing are there." - James 3:16

Introduction

This chapter chronicles the complex series of events leading to the decline and eventual demise of the Azusa Street Revival. It explores internal conflicts, doctrinal disputes, and the impact of leadership changes on the movement's trajectory.

Word of Wisdom

"Pentecost means to live right in the 13th chapter of First Corinthians, which is the standard." - William Seymour

"THE DECLINE, SECOND SHOWER, AND DEMISE"

Main Theme

The chapter delves into the decline of the Azusa Street Revival, highlighting internal conflicts, leadership challenges, and doctrinal disagreements that contributed to its eventual demise.

Key Points

- The Azusa Street Mission was incorporated in 1907, marking a shift in its organizational structure.

- By 1908, the revival became a global phenomenon, but internal conflicts and changes began to surface.

- Serious internal challenges arose over financial transparency and doctrinal issues.

- The revival faced a major setback with the departure of Clara Lum, who took the ministry's publication to Portland.

- William Durham's arrival in 1911 brought doctrinal disputes and further division.

- Racial and ideological divisions increasingly strained the unity that had characterized the early revival.

Key Themes

- The incorporation of the Azusa Street Mission and the purchase of its building represented a transition from a spontaneous spiritual movement to a more structured organization. This change

marked the beginning of internal conflicts and a shift in the revival's direction.
- The departure of Clara Lum with the ministry's publication to Portland significantly weakened the Azusa Street Mission's influence and outreach, leading to a decline in support and participation.
- William Durham's introduction of the "Finished Work" doctrine challenged existing beliefs about sanctification, creating doctrinal rifts and dividing the community, which accelerated the decline of the revival.
- Racial and ideological divisions, particularly in the context of Durham's teachings, began to undermine the inclusive and diverse nature of the Azusa Street Revival, leading to its fragmentation.
- The revival's decline was not solely due to external factors but also stemmed from internal disagreements, leadership disputes, and shifting theological interpretations that eroded its foundational unity.

Conclusion

"The Decline, Second Shower, and Demise" offers a comprehensive look at the complex factors contributing to the decline of the Azusa Street Revival. From organizational changes to doctrinal disputes and leadership challenges, the chapter provides insights into how a powerful spiritual movement can be impacted by internal dynamics

"THE DECLINE, SECOND SHOWER, AND DEMISE"

and external pressures. The story of Azusa Street serves as a cautionary tale about the importance of maintaining unity, doctrinal clarity, and humble leadership in sustaining a spiritual revival.

CHAPTER 13

"THE AZUSA STREET LEGACY"

Bible Verse

"Not by might, nor by power, but by my Spirit, saith the Lord of hosts." - Zechariah 4:6

Introduction

This chapter explores the complex legacy of the Azusa Street Revival, focusing on the challenges and changes faced by its leader, William Seymour, and the impact of racial dynamics on the movement.

Word of Wisdom

"The world was his parish." - Reflecting on William Seymour's global influence in the Pentecostal movement.

"THE AZUSA STREET LEGACY"

Main Theme

The chapter discusses the pivotal role of William Seymour in the Azusa Street Revival, highlighting the racial and doctrinal challenges he faced and the significant impact of his leadership on the global Pentecostal movement.

Key Points

- Key white figures, including Parham and Durham, attempted to take control of Seymour's ministry, impacting its direction.

- Lum and Crawford, also white, succeeded in diverting the mission's influence by relocating its publication to Portland in 1908.

- The Azusa Street Mission's leadership was later limited to people of color due to growing racism and internal conflicts.

- Seymour's final years were marked by struggles to maintain the mission, with reduced attendance and influence.

- The demolition of the Azusa Street Mission building and the subsequent legal battles over its legacy signified the end of an era.

Key Themes

- The leadership changes and doctrinal disputes within the Azusa Street Mission, primarily influenced by white leaders, deeply affected Seymour and the

movement's direction. These changes not only altered the mission's trajectory but also led to a significant decline in its influence and unity.
- The decision to limit leadership roles to people of color was a response to increasing racial tensions and internal conflicts. This decision, while aimed at maintaining peace, highlighted the racial challenges within the Pentecostal movement and reflected the broader societal issues of the time.
- The later years of Seymour's life were characterized by diminishing influence and resources, demonstrating the fragility of spiritual movements and the challenges of sustaining momentum over time.
- The demolition of the Azusa Street Mission building and the subsequent controversies around its legacy symbolized the end of the physical presence of a movement that had a profound global impact. This event marked the transition of the Azusa Street Revival from a physical location to a historical and spiritual legacy.
- The Azusa Street Revival's impact on the global Pentecostal movement was profound, with its emphasis on racial equality, spiritual empowerment, and charismatic worship influencing countless individuals and churches worldwide. Despite its internal challenges, the revival's legacy continues to shape Christian practices and beliefs.

Conclusion

"The Azusa Street Legacy" chapter provides a comprehensive examination of the challenges, changes, and enduring impact of the Azusa Street Revival under William Seymour's leadership. It highlights the interplay of racial dynamics, doctrinal disputes, and leadership struggles in shaping the movement's trajectory. Despite its decline, the legacy of the Azusa Street Revival remains a significant chapter in the history of modern Pentecostalism, remembered for its pioneering spirit and its push for racial equality and spiritual renewal.

CHAPTER 14

"THE PILGRIMS OF AZUSA STREET"

Bible Verse

"For we are God's fellow workers; you are God's field, God's building." - 1 Corinthians 3:9

Introduction

This chapter delves into the spread of the Pentecostal movement from Azusa Street, highlighting the key individuals who carried the revival's message across the United States and beyond, creating a legacy of global Pentecostalism.

Word of Wisdom

"The people that receive the baptism seem so happy, they remind me of our people at home." - Reflecting the joy and transformation experienced by those touched by the Azusa Street Revival.

"THE PILGRIMS OF AZUSA STREET"

Main Theme

The chapter focuses on the influential figures who visited Azusa Street and became instrumental in spreading Pentecostalism globally, emphasizing their diverse backgrounds and the spread of the movement to various regions.

Key Points

• Azusa Street visitors, known as "the pilgrims of Los Angeles," played crucial roles in spreading Pentecostalism worldwide.

• Prominent figures like Florence Crawford, Glenn Cook, and William Durham founded Pentecostal movements in various regions.

• Children also experienced the Pentecostal baptism, indicating a widespread and diverse impact.

• William Seymour himself traveled extensively, evangelizing and establishing churches.

• Pentecostal denominations like the Assemblies of God and Church of God in Christ trace their origins to Azusa Street.

Key Themes

- The Azusa Street Revival catalyzed a global movement, with "pilgrims" traveling far and wide to spread the Pentecostal message. These individuals, transformed by their experiences at Azusa Street, took the

revival's essence to new communities, sparking widespread spiritual awakening.
- The involvement of children in the Pentecostal movement was remarkable. Their participation in speaking in tongues and preaching demonstrated the revival's profound and inclusive nature, impacting individuals regardless of age.
- The establishment of major Pentecostal denominations can be directly traced to Azusa Street. The foundation and growth of these denominations highlight the lasting impact of the revival on global Christianity.
- The spread of Pentecostalism often encountered resistance and skepticism. Yet, despite challenges, the movement's message of spiritual empowerment and charismatic worship gained significant traction.
- The doctrinal evolution within the Pentecostal movement, particularly debates over baptism and the nature of the Holy Trinity, shows the dynamic and evolving nature of early Pentecostal theology.

Conclusion

"The Pilgrims of Azusa Street" chapter underscores the far-reaching influence of the Azusa Street Revival. It highlights the individuals who carried the flame of Pentecostalism from Los Angeles to the rest of the world, planting the seeds of a global spiritual movement. Their journeys, challenges, and successes illustrate the profound impact of Azusa Street, making it a cornerstone in the history of modern Christianity.

CHAPTER 15

"BEGINNING OF A WORLDWIDE REVIVAL"

Bible Verse
"And this gospel of the kingdom will be preached in the whole world as a testimony to all nations, and then the end will come." - Matthew 24:14

Introduction

"Beginning of a Worldwide Revival" explores the rapid global spread of the Pentecostal movement originating from Azusa Street, highlighting the critical role of missionaries and the profound influence of the Apostolic Faith publication.

Word of Wisdom

"The Lord showed me a few years ago that out of California would come a movement that would startle the world, and here is the prophecy fulfilled." - Reflecting

"BEGINNING OF A WORLDWIDE REVIVAL"

the global impact and fulfillment of the Azusa Street Revival.

Main Theme

This chapter focuses on the far-reaching influence of the Azusa Street Revival as it sparked a global Pentecostal movement through the work of missionaries and the distribution of the Apostolic Faith publication.

Key Points

• The Azusa Street Revival rapidly spread across the globe, influencing various regions and cultures.

• The Apostolic Faith publication played a crucial role in disseminating Pentecostal teachings worldwide.

• T.B. Barratt, influenced by the revival, was pivotal in spreading Pentecostalism in Europe.

• Many missionaries from Azusa Street ventured into international fields, facing both successes and challenges.

• Veteran missionaries revitalized their efforts after experiencing the revival at Azusa Street.

Key Themes

- The Azusa Street Revival transcended cultural and geographical boundaries, demonstrating its universal appeal and

adaptability. Missionaries who visited Azusa Street returned to their fields or ventured into new ones, taking with them a renewed spiritual fervor and Pentecostal practices.
- The Apostolic Faith publication became an essential tool for spreading the revival's message. Its reach extended far beyond the physical gatherings at Azusa Street, touching lives and sparking revivals in distant lands through its written testimonies and teachings.
- The influence of key figures like T.B. Barratt and the Garrs highlights the individual impact of the revival. Their journeys from Azusa Street to Europe and Asia respectively, underline the personal transformation and dedication to spreading the Pentecostal message.
- The varied experiences of Azusa Street missionaries reflect both the triumphs and trials of early Pentecostal missions. While some faced disillusionment or opposition, others successfully adapted and thrived in their mission fields.
- The establishment of significant Pentecostal centers and denominations worldwide can be traced back to the Azusa Street Revival. This demonstrates the revival's lasting legacy in shaping the global Pentecostal landscape.

Conclusion

"Beginning of a Worldwide Revival" captures the essence of the Azusa Street Revival as a seminal

"BEGINNING OF A WORLDWIDE REVIVAL"

event in the history of global Christianity. Its influence, carried by passionate individuals and through powerful publications, ignited a worldwide Pentecostal movement that reshaped religious expression and community across continents. The chapter celebrates this extraordinary legacy, emphasizing the revival's transformative power and far-reaching impact.

CHAPTER 16

"UNLOCKING AZUSA FIRE BY RICK JOYNER"

Bible Verse

"But God chose the foolish things of the world to shame the wise; God chose the weak things of the world to shame the strong." - 1 Corinthians 1:27

Introduction

"Unlocking Azusa Fire" by Rick Joyner positions the Azusa Street Revival as a pivotal event in modern Christianity, likening its impact to the apostolic era. Joyner emphasizes the humble beginnings of the revival and its global influence, suggesting it foreshadows an even greater movement of God.

Word of Wisdom

"God will do it again, only bigger!" - Capturing the spirit of anticipation for a future revival surpassing Azusa Street's impact.

Main Theme

The book explores the Azusa Street Revival's profound impact on global Christianity and its role as a harbinger for a future, unprecedented move of God.

Key Points

- The Azusa Street Revival is likened to an act of God that would have featured in the Book of Acts.

- This revival is seen as a precursor to an even more significant global movement, the final "harvest."

- The revival's impact was felt worldwide, transforming church life and setting a course for modern Christianity.

- Azusa Street's leadership, particularly William Seymour, demonstrated humility and a profound reliance on the Holy Spirit.

- The revival served as a restoration of lost Christian truths and practices, igniting a worldwide Pentecostal movement.

Key Themes

- The revival's global influence and significance are attributed to its humble origins and divine orchestration. The revival began in a modest setting, demonstrating God's preference for using the humble and weak to manifest His power.

- The Azusa Street Revival initiated a series of restorative movements within Christianity, contributing to a significant transformation in church dynamics and the widespread adoption of Pentecostal practices.
- The leadership at Azusa Street, particularly William Seymour, is highlighted for its humility and reliance on the Holy Spirit. Seymour's leadership style, emphasizing openness to the Spirit's guidance, was instrumental in fostering the revival's environment.
- The revival's impact on global Christianity is underscored as pivotal for understanding the church's modern era. The Azusa Street Revival set foundational principles for contemporary Christian movements and denominations.
- Joyner proposes that the Azusa Street Revival is a foreshadowing of a future, more extensive global spiritual movement. This anticipated movement is expected to surpass the impact of Azusa Street, marking the greatest move of God in history.

Conclusion

"Unlocking Azusa Fire" asserts the Azusa Street Revival as a transformative event in Christian history, one that reinvigorated the church and anticipated a future global spiritual awakening. Joyner's analysis serves as both a tribute to the revival's historical significance and a prophetic anticipation of an even more profound move of God in the future.

FAITH AND FLAME PRESS
IGNITING THE FLAMES OF FAITH

Faith and Flame Press is a Christian book publishing company that is passionate about igniting the flames of faith in the hearts of readers around the world. Our mission is to publish books that inspire, enlighten, and uplift the spirit, and help readers deepen their understanding of their faith and spirituality.

At Faith and Flame Press, we believe that books have the power to transform lives and to shape the world we live in. That's why we are committed to publishing books that are not only spiritually uplifting but also intellectually stimulating, well-researched, and thought-provoking.

www.ingramcontent.com/pod-product-compliance
Lightning Source LLC
Chambersburg PA
CBHW070209100426
42743CB00013B/3112